Black and White Photography in the Digital Age

I0390449

David Bigwood, LRPS

formerly Editor The Black and White Enthusiast

CONTENTS

1   Introduction   3

2   Basic Conversion   4

3   Colour or Black and White?   10

4   Photoshop's Duotone   20

5   Black and White Variations   28

6   Photoshop Magic   39

7   About the Author   46

INTRODUCTION

As someone who spent many happy years watching images appear in dishes of developer by the glow of the red darkroom safelight, I still have a hankering in this digital age for black and white photography. And it is somewhat incongruous that the digital camera has actually made it easier to produce black and white images than it was in film days. Then if I wanted to capture both colour and black and white, I needed to have two cameras with me with one loaded with black and white film and the other with colour. And, if the light deteriorated during a shoot, I had either to give up or load a faster film if I had one with me.

Now, I just use one camera and shoot in RAW format in colour and vary the ISO according to the light level for each shot. Why RAW? Simply because I end up with as much material available to me as my sensor can handle without the camera making decisions about what should be kept and what thrown away. That job should be mine and mine alone. Once I have the pictures on my computer, I can then decide how I want them to appear and process them accordingly.

This book is dedicated to showing how first class black and white images can be produced from the colour pictures you have captured on your digital camera.

Basic conversion from colour to black and white

As with so many procedures in Photoshop there are differing methods to get to the same end result. Converting colour images to black and white is no exception. Here are some of them.

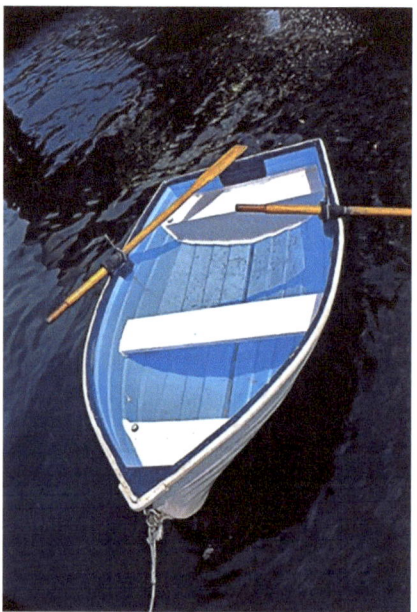

Original colour picture

Grayscale Mode

The simplest and quickest way was how I started and that was just to change the mode in Photoshop from RGB to Grayscale. I opened the picture, went to 'Image' in the Menu Bar and selected 'Mode' then selected 'Grayscale' from the drop down menu. This brought up a dialogue box asking if I wanted to discard all colour information. I clicked 'OK' and the job was done. I was then able to adjust the monochrome image to my liking. It couldn't get any easier. 'Easy-peasey,' as Jamie Oliver would say.

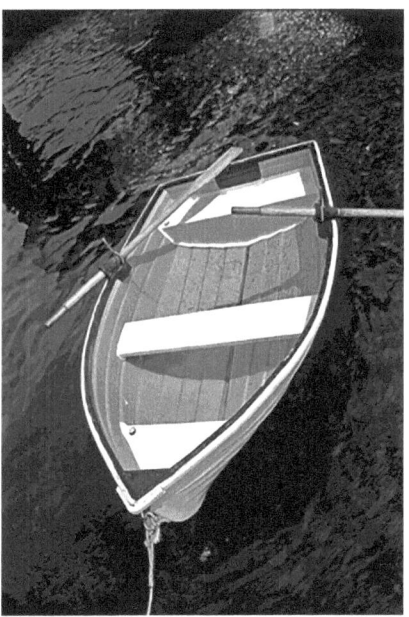

Desaturate Method

As easy is the use of the 'Desaturate' command. With the original colour picture open, go to 'Image' select 'Adjustments' and 'Desaturate' from the drop down menu. The result is very similar to the Grayscale method and can also be achieved by going to 'Hue/Saturate' and reducing the 'Saturation' slider to -100.

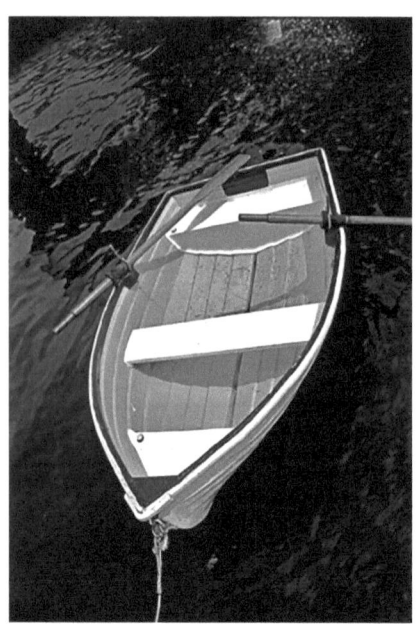

Channel Mixer Method

Now we come to a slightly more complicated method but one that gives a higher control than the previous two. Once again, with the original colour picture open, go to 'Image' and select 'Adjustments' then select 'Channel Mixer' from the drop down menu. This will bring up the Channel Mixer dialogue box with sliders for the Red, Green and Blue channels. When opened the sliders will be set for 100% red and 0% for the other two channels. Before you do anything, select the Monochrome box at the bottom left of the dialogue box. Then have a look at the image with 100% for each of the other two colours in turn and 0% for the rest. The results will depend upon the majority of colours in the original. You may find that one of the channels suits you perfectly, in which case you can ignore the other two by leaving them at 0 and click on 'OK'.

However, it will probably be the case that you can get a better result by mixing bits of each channel. I start generally by reducing the Red to about 50 or 60 and increasing Green to 20 to 30 and the Blue to whatever makes up 100 — you don't have to end up with 100 but the results are normally better if you do. Once I have made the initial changes, it is a matter of trial and error to come up with the best result.

The Constant slider allows adjustments of the finished image — sliding to the left produces a darker result and to the right, a lighter one. I have found that I rarely adjust this.

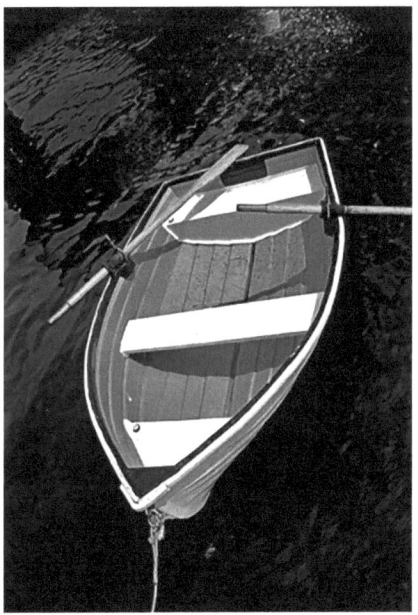

LAB Mode

Another method that produces generally good results is to use the LAB Mode. With the colour image open, go to 'Image' and select 'Mode' then choose 'Lab color'. In the Layers Window, select 'Channels' (if Channels is not visible, go to 'Windows' in the top menu and select it) which will give you four channels, LAB, Lightness, A and B. Select the Lightness channel. Go to 'Image>Mode>Grayscale' click 'OK' in the dialogue box that asks whether you want to discard the other channels and you have a monochrome image to adjust to your satisfaction.

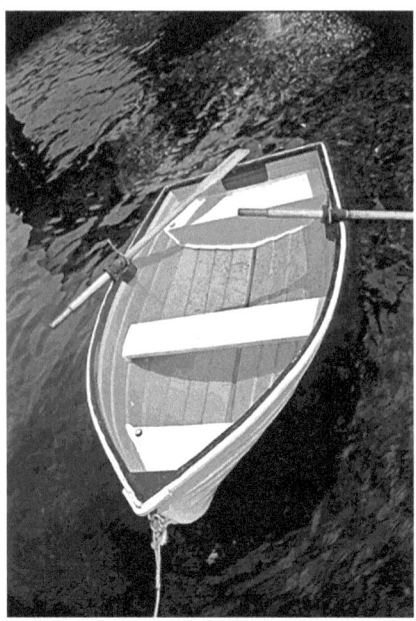

Any one of the completed operations above will provide a useable monochrome image. However, all require additional work to make them into more than just a basic monochrome picture.

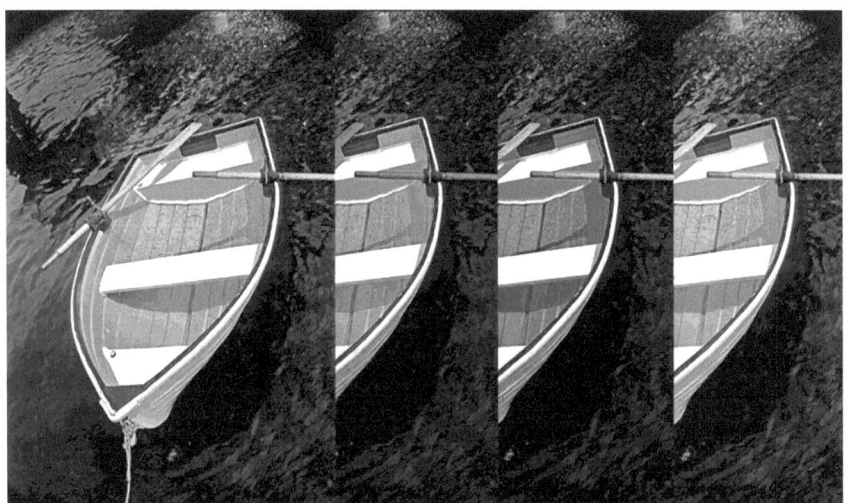

From left to right, Grayscale, De-saturate, Channel Mix, and LAB

As you have seen, and as with so many operations in Photoshop, it is possible to get to an end result in various ways and the ones I have outlined are not the only ones that will provide a conversion to monochrome. Some swear by one method and some by another. Just find one that suits you but be aware there are alternatives. In the next chapter you will find that I use another method available in Adobe Camera Raw (available as a free download from www.adobe.com).

Colour or Black and White?

I live in the Snowy Mountains of New South Wales, one of the many very photogenic places in Australia which is evidenced by the number of top class photographers who live and work here with two photography galleries in Jindabyne and nearby. I, too, would like to be able to sell some of my images but how do I manage against such strong competition? I've been successful with an unusual picture of a group of kangaroos, some with joeys, in the snow which has been purchased as a print several times with one hanging in a Canadian hospital and has been also a successful postcard but I cannot count on being able to capture 'unusual' pictures consistently.

I was pondering this problem recently when I came across a new book on digital black and white and the penny finally dropped. The local galleries are filled predominantly with fine colour prints so why not go back to my successful days of film when I had a darkroom and regularly entered the National exhibitions held in Australia and gained a first and a number of Highly Commended awards for my black and white prints, a panel of which also gained me the Licentiateship of the Royal Photographic Society? That could be the way for me to differentiate myself from the competition.

Just after the 2009 ski season ended the mountains had their biggest dump of snow of the winter and I was quick to head up the hill to Charlotte Pass where I stumbled through the deep snow looking for pictures, in particular those that could be turned into black and white images. I eventually found a typically tortured and twisted snow gum that looked as if it would fill the bill. With my camera on my tripod and the legs firmly pressed into the deep snow I shot the RAW image at 1/100 second at f22 with ISO 100 using a wide angle lens.

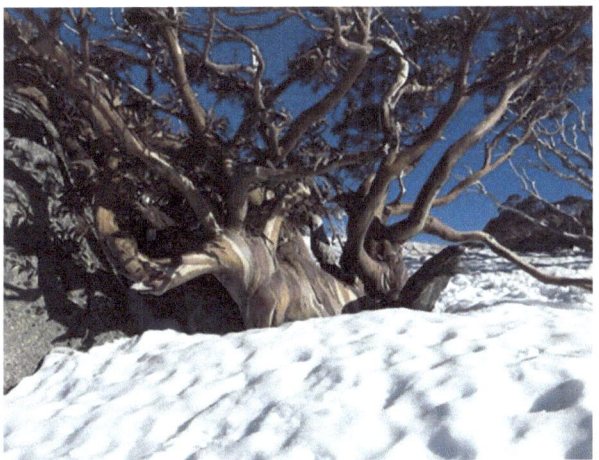

Even if I want to end up with a black and white print, I still shoot in RAW colour as I still need colour images for my freelance photography business and the author of the book I found considers that it is possible to get better results from converting a colour image than from shooting in monochrome mode. I use RAW to capture and retain all the detail in the image and to prevent the camera making decisions and discarding information without my say so.

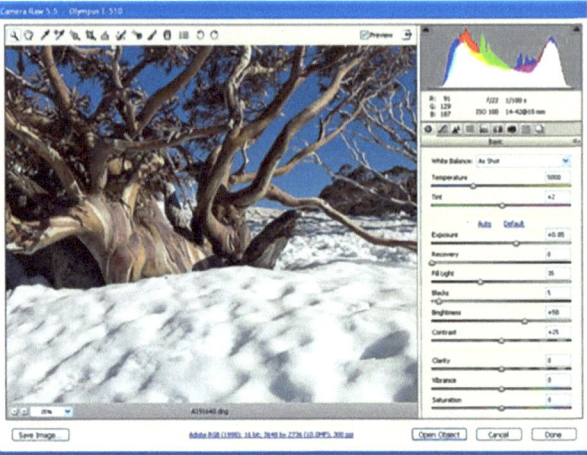

Figure 1

Once the image was on my computer, I opened it in Adobe Camera Raw (figure 1). The histogram showed that there was no clipping of highlights or shadows (I always check the histogram after exposing and will use the exposure compensation facility until I get an acceptable result) so I moved straight to the HSL/Grayscale icon and clicked on the 'Convert to Grayscale' box (figure 2). Beneath this box there is the facility to adjust a number of colours and this is where I went to work (figure 3). Having taken into account the colours in the captured shot I was able to have a fair idea of which colours needed to be adjusted. Then it was a case of tweaking until I felt the image was the best I could make it at this stage. Do make sure that you have a properly calibrated monitor otherwise when you print, you may end up with some unexpected results.

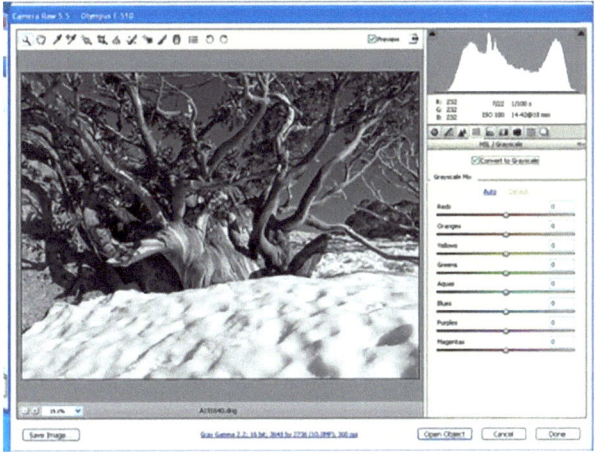

Figure 2

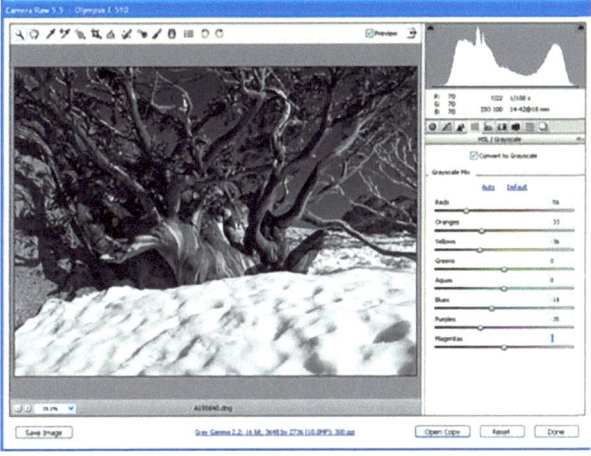

Figure 3

If you do not shoot in RAW or are using a scanned image shot on film, you can use the Black and White adjustment layer in Photoshop which will enable you to do the same process as in Adobe Camera Raw.

Now it was time to open the image as a Smart Object in Photoshop (figure 4) and continue with the fine tuning. As is my custom, I began with a minute Curves adjustment (figure 5). On this occasion, the highlights were adjusted slightly while the shadows were untouched.

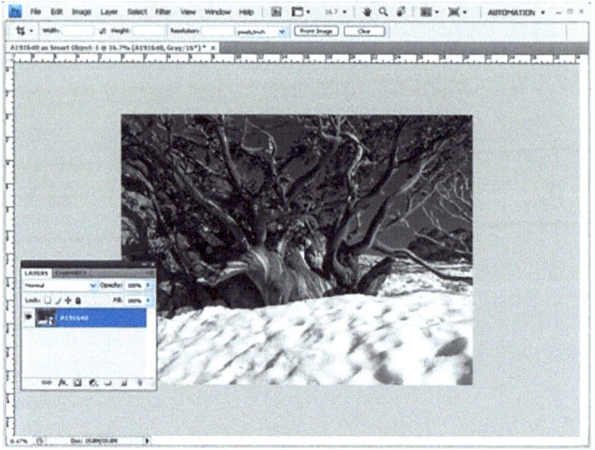

Figure 4

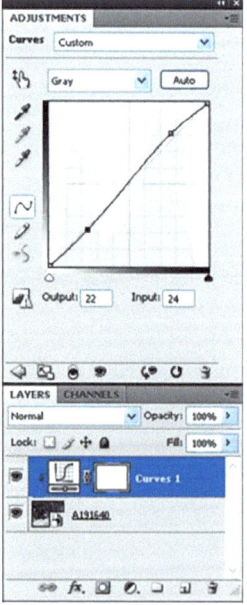

Figure 5

I considered that the tree trunk was too dark so used another curve to lighten it (figure 6). When using this curve, I only concentrated on the tree and did not worry that other parts of the image were looking wrong. The reason for this was that I was about to use a mask so that only the tree trunk was affected by the adjustment. I clicked on the white rectangle against Curves 2 (a mask) and pressed Control + I to fill that mask with black and hide the adjustments I had just made (figure 7). I then selected the brush from the tool box, adjusted the size as appropriate and with a soft edge chosen and the foreground colour set to white began to paint the tree until it looked as I wanted it (figure 8). You can see the area that I worked on appearing as a white section in the black mask.

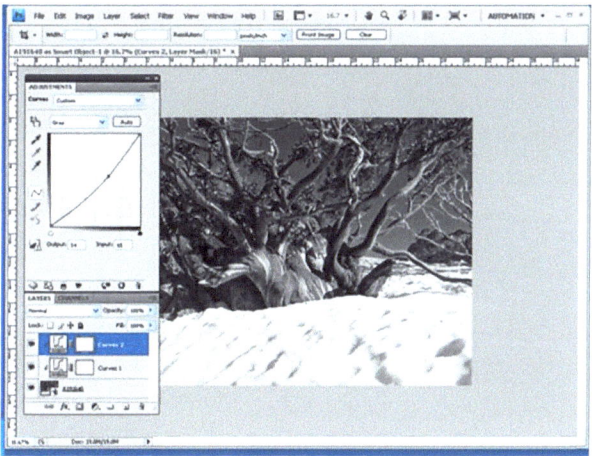

Figure 6

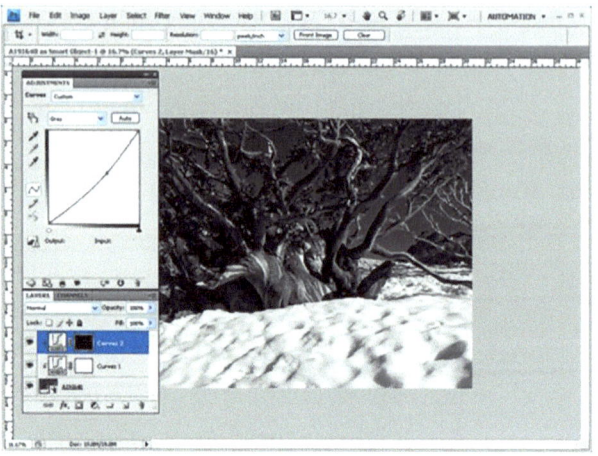

Figure 7

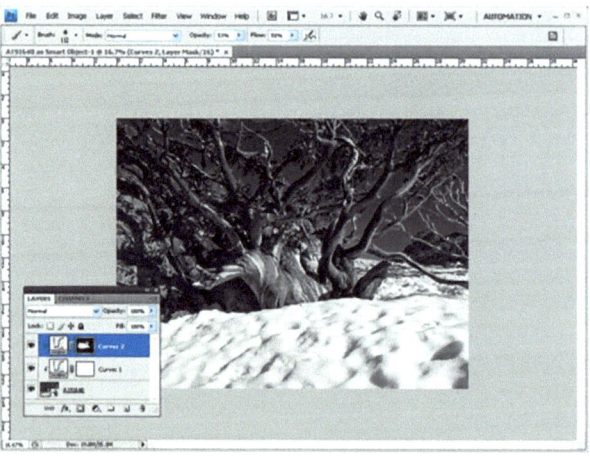

Figure 8

I decided that the snow at the base of the picture tended to grab the eye so resorted to an old darkroom technique of burning it in slightly. I opened a new layer, selected the area to be darkened using the lasso tool and then filled it with black from the paint bucket. The opacity was then reduced to 13% and the area deselected (figure 9). I repeated this burning on the other three sides using a new layer for each with the opacity adjusted as required.

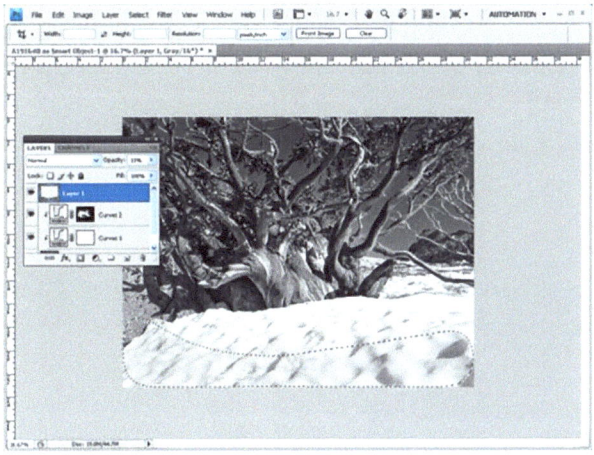

Figure 9

It was time to sit back and take a good look at my picture. Eventually, I decided that some more contrast was needed so I took advantage of one of the great facilities offered by working with Smart Objects and double clicked on the image on the Background layer which took me back to Adobe Camera Raw where I was able to adjust the brightness and the contrast (figure 10). Clicking 'OK' returned me to the Smart Object in Photoshop with the adjustments made.

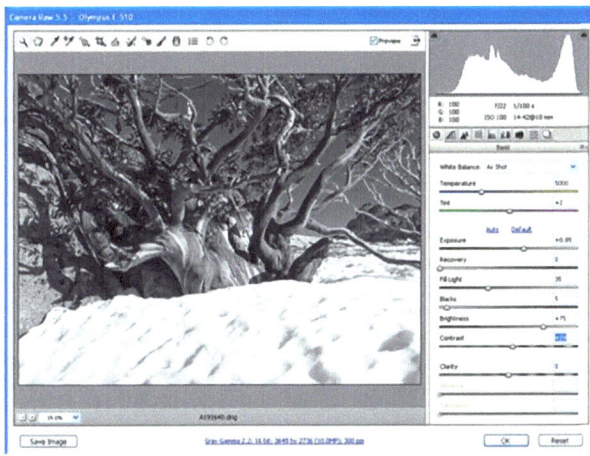

Figure 10

Figure 11 shows the final image with all its adjustments. This I save with all its layers because if I want to tweak any of the adjustments I have made all I have to do is open the image, select the layer I want to change and adjust it. Note that it is in its unsharpened state as I save the sharpening for the final image when I prepare it for printing and have adjusted the size.

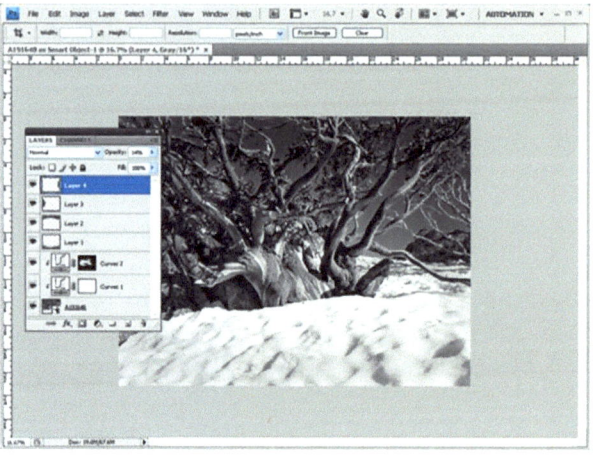

Figure 11

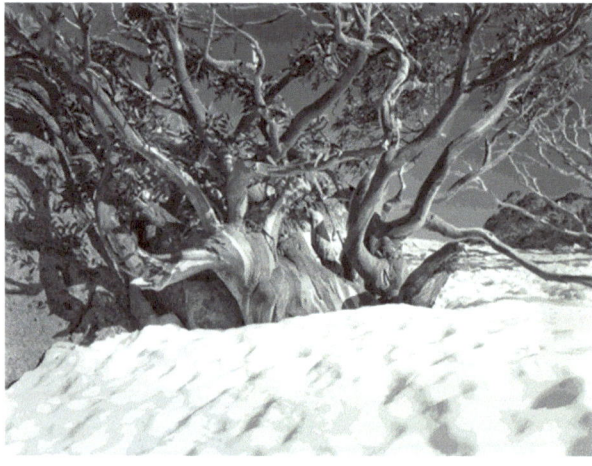

The process described above retains as much of the information captured in RAW as I can. My whole aim is to avoid destructive processes where possible.

For further detailed explanation of the black and white process, I recommend *Black and White Pipeline — converting digital colour into striking grayscale images* by Ted Dillard published by Lark Books (ISBN 978-1-60059-400-7).

Will my strategy enable me to sell some of my prints? Only time will tell. But, if nothing else, it has provided me with the opportunity to return to my first love of black and white photography.

Add Some Snap with Photoshop's Duotone

I have been reasonably happy with the process that I have used to produce most of my black and white prints on my inkjet printer whether from converted colour images or scanned negatives. But I am not entirely happy when it comes to prints intended for hanging as there is a nagging impression that they just aren't up to the standard that I achieved when sloshing around in chemicals in the darkroom. Then the prints intended for exhibition would have received a final bath in dilute selenium toner to produce the snap that real blacks make to a print.

Not that I mourn the passing of the selenium bath — it was not a friendly chemical to have around and it did stink. But it did the job that I asked of it.

Many versions of Photoshop ago I tried the duotone mode of preparing images for printing but it wasn't a success — not, I hasten to add because of Photoshop but how I handled it in my far less expert days.

However, the search for that extra bit of quality in my monochrome prints has dragged me back to the duotone mode. And, yes, I can see the subtle improvements. Subtle is the word but then it also was the word with selenium if it was just enhanced blacks that you were after.

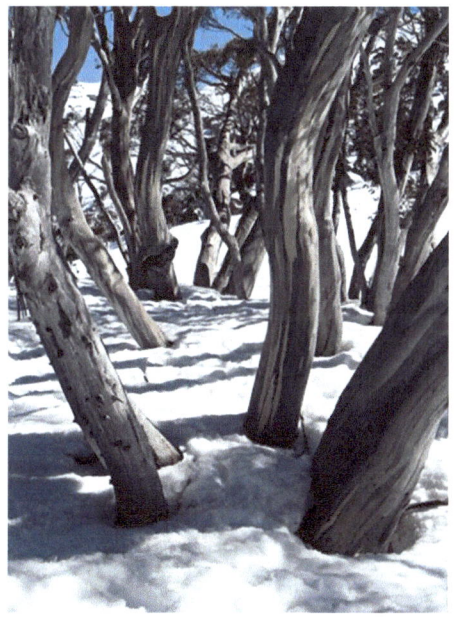

Figure 1

So, how does duotone work? Let's start with a digital colour image (figure 1) and convert it to monochrome using whichever method you like (figure 2). As you can only access the duotone mode from a grayscale image at 8 bits you have to ensure that it is in 8 bit mode (Image/Mode/8 bit) change the Mode from RGB to Grayscale, and click 'Discard Color Information' when it comes up in a dialogue box.

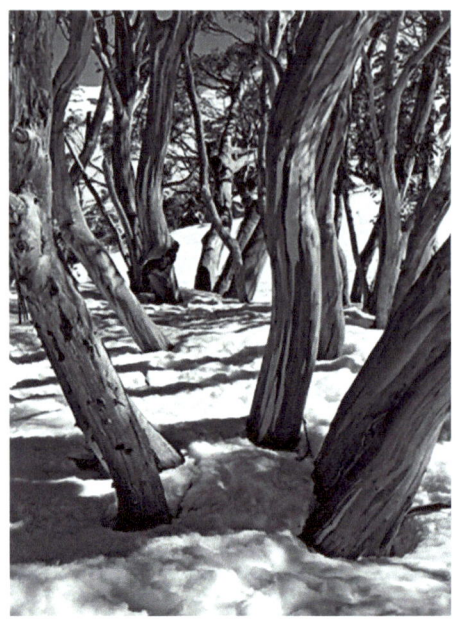

Figure 2

Now you can change the Mode to Duotone which brings up the dialogue box shown in figure 3. If the Type shows 'Monotone' click on the drop down menu and choose 'Duotone'. Working in this dialogue box is the crux of the whole duotone operation so expect to spend some time tweaking.

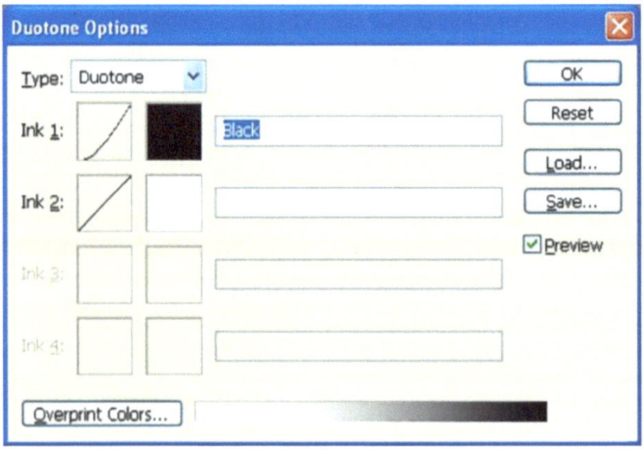

Figure 3

When set to 'Duotone', the Duotone dialogue box has a square filled with black with a white one below it. You can leave the black alone but you need to click on the white so that you can choose the second ink colour. You are offered a myriad of colours to choose from and a number of sets under the drop down Book menu (figure 4). Personal preference and the desired result have a great bearing on what you choose so it is likely that you will spend some time selecting and discarding various colours until you find one that satisfies you.

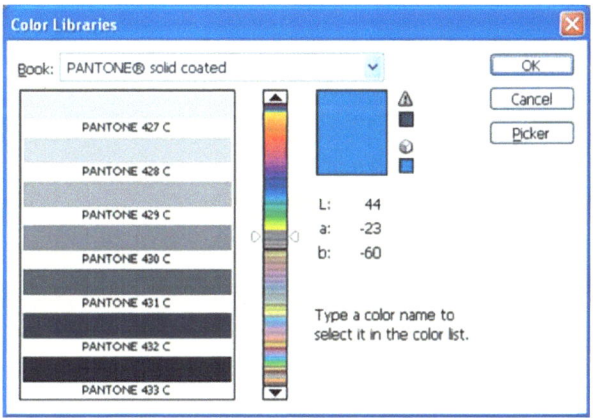

Figure 4

For my picture, I decided on the Pantone 7533C, quite a dark brown which would suit the bark of the trees, from the Pantone Solid Coated set.

The decision on colour is not the finish for this dialogue box as you will find when you click on the box to the left of either of the colour boxes and open the Curves control. I generally start with the second ink and only tweak the curves for the black box if I think it might improve the final result. As you will see from figure 5 the Curves box allows you an infinite number of variations which you can implement by dragging the curves line or by typing in numbers in the percentages boxes until you are satisfied with the result. I generally try dragging the curve and watching the result. If, as often happens, I end up with some bizarre looking picture after dragging I can go to the percentage box I have been working with and delete the number to return to an appropriate looking image before I start dragging again. The adjustment of the Curves decides how much of the colour you have chosen is applied to each part of the image with 0% being pure white, 50% mid-grey and 100% the deepest shadow. As you can see, I didn't want much of the second ink applied up to about mid-grey and then a smooth curve increasing the amount until the 100% mark.

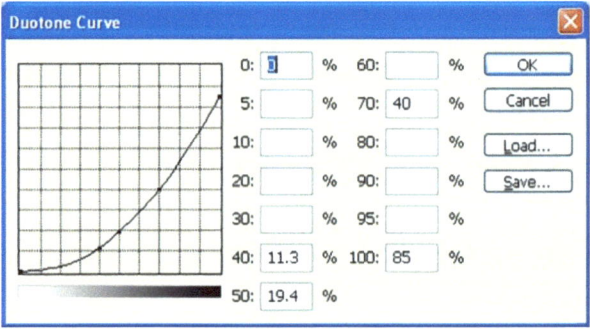

Figure 5

To print, you will have to return the Mode to RGB. I find that sometimes a little judicious tweaking of Shadows/Highlights and Exposure together with sharpening before printing can add just a bit of snap to the final print.

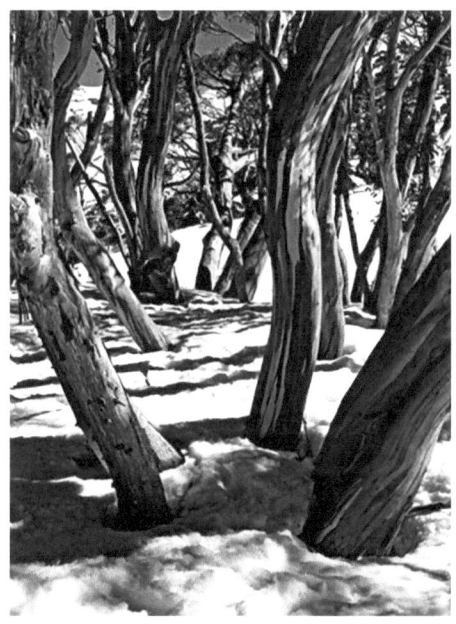

You will have noticed the extra two colour boxes in the Duotone dialogue box. These are for even more subtle improvements using three colours (Tritones) or four (Quadtones). These are activated by choosing the appropriate Type from the drop down menu but I do suggest that you master the Duotone process before venturing further.

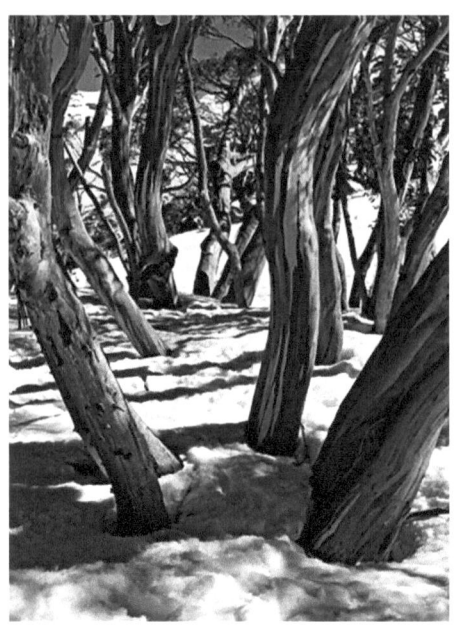

Tritone print

In the Duotone dialogue box you will also see a button marked 'Load'. By clicking on this you will bring up a number of Photoshop pre-set duotones. When starting, it is not a bad idea to try these out and use the one that suits your image best as a basis for your own tweaking of the curves.

What are the appropriate colours to use for the second ink? While individual preferences have a lot to do with the answer, there are certain colours that do produce great looking blacks. Blue added to black makes for a good depth of colour and produces a cool looking result while brown or even red adds warmth to the picture. Yellow enables a sepia toned print to be replicated and grey gives a neutral black. Then there are the greens which in moderation can work very well in the cool part of the spectrum. And so it goes on. In fact, individual preferences probably have everything to do with the answer. Experiment and enjoy.

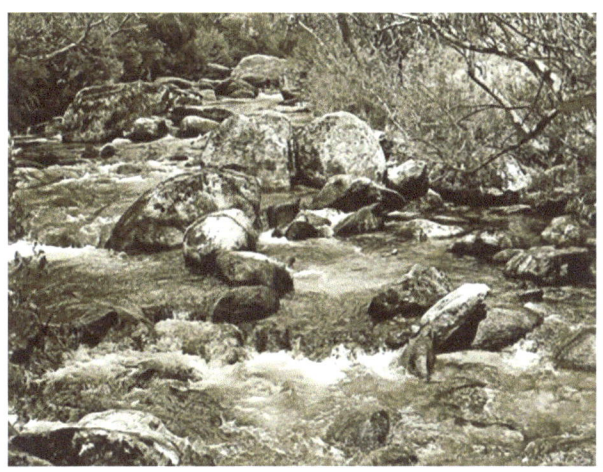

Duotone sepia print

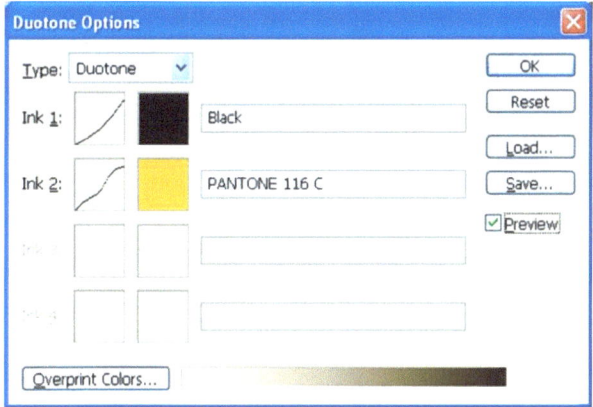

Inks chosen for sepia print above

Black and White Variations

Making pictures and storing them on your computer is great but the ultimate must be the making of fine prints of some of your best shots that are worthy of hanging on your wall. I have been doing this recently as I have been lucky enough to have a bookshop and a Post Office keen to present some of my images for sale. Interestingly, the images that are selling are mostly black and white which has made me think back to my darkroom days and try to simulate some of the effects I achieved there in Photoshop.

What came immediately to mind were sepia, selenium, and split toning — these I had tried with varying degrees of success but now I could even attempt simulating lith printing.

As with many things in Photoshop, there are a number of ways to achieve the toning of black and white prints. I spent some hours trying many of the toning techniques and what I include in this article are those that I have found that work well for me.

All the processes I describe are able to be done using the drop down menus at the top of your screen but I do as much as I can in the

Layers palette as I can easily see just what adjustments I have made and can return to any one of them to tweak it if necessary. I also save all the adjustment layers so that I can tweak at a later date if I want to. To access the adjustment layers in the Layers palette just click on the half black and half white circle at the bottom of the box and select what you need.

Sepia

Sepia was the easiest toning that I did. Photoshop even provides a pre-set for doing it in its Photo Filters. If starting from a colour original, convert it to black and white using whichever conversion process suits you. On a new adjustment layer select Photo Filter (If using the top menu, Image>Adjustment>Photo Filter). In the Photo Filter dialogue box go to the drop down menu and select Sepia then use the Density slider to adjust the tone to your liking.

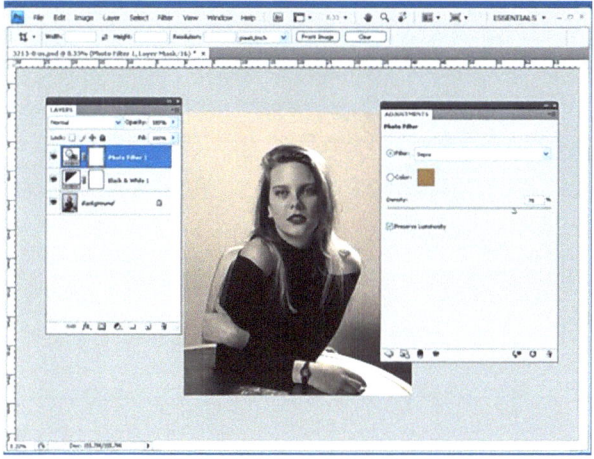

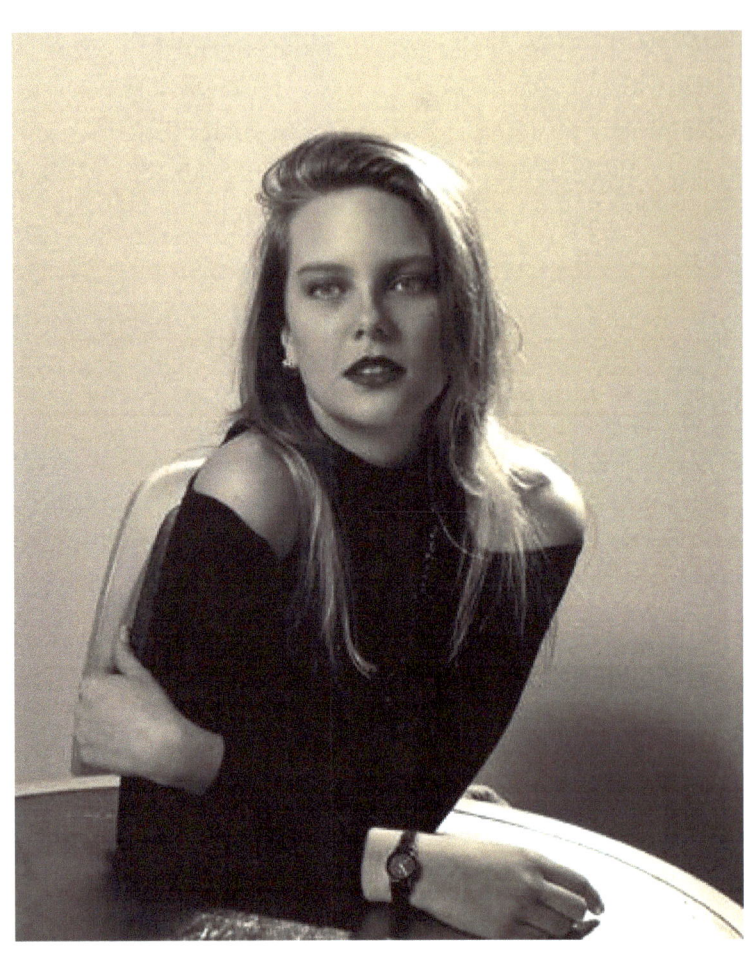

Sepia toning using Photo Filter

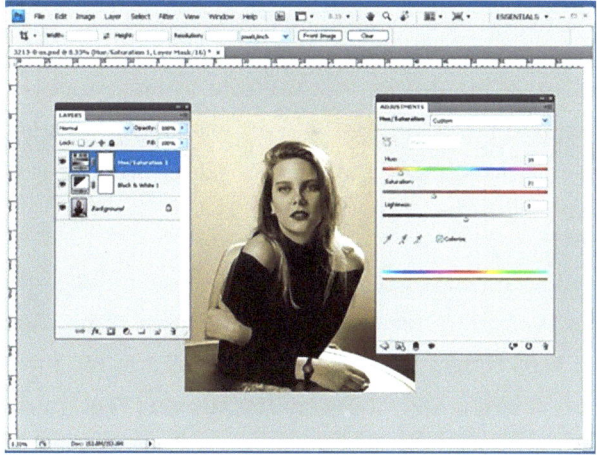

You can also achieve the sepia effect by using the Hue/Saturation adjustment (Image>Adjustment>Hue Saturation). In the Hue Saturation dialogue box select 'Colorize' then adjust the hue and saturation sliders until satisfied with the colour. Very easy.

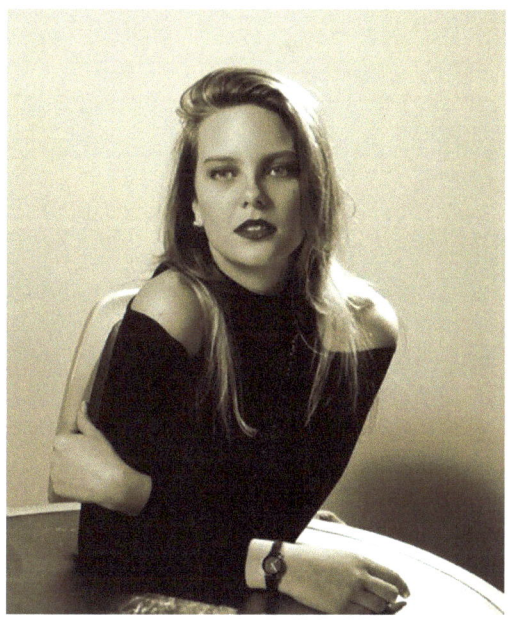

Sepia toning using Hue/Saturation

Split Toning

I then spent some time testing out the split toning process. As so often happened in the darkroom when I was trying out a different process, I went through a fair amount of paper but that is to be expected when experimenting.

Start with your black and white image and open a Hue/Saturation Adjustment Layer go to Select>Color Range (this time I had to resort to the top of screen menu as Color Range is not in the Layers palette). Select 'Highlights' from the drop down menu in the Color Range dialogue box and click 'OK' which will result in a Layer Mask being made in the Hue/Saturation Adjustment Layer so that any alterations you make in the Hue/Saturation box will only apply to the highlights. In the Hue/Saturation box, tick 'Colorize' and then use the hue and saturation sliders to produce the colour you want.

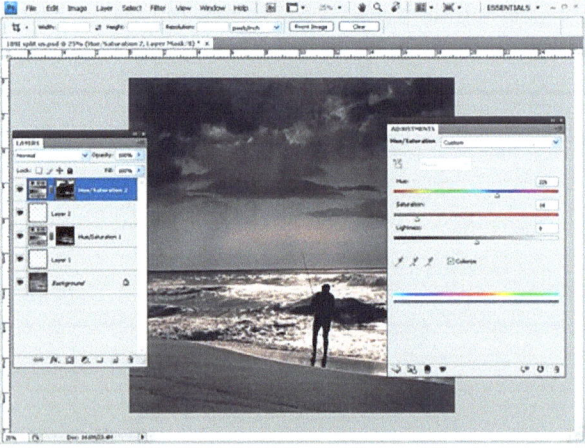

Open another Hue/Saturation Adjustment Layer and repeat the above but this time select 'Shadows' in the Color Range box. The new Layer Mask will allow any adjustments to affect the shadows only. If necessary you can now go back to the highlights layer and tweak it. This is why I use the Layers palette box.

If using the top menu, when you choose highlights or shadows in the

Color Range box and click 'OK' the marching ants will appear to show what you have selected. Then go to Image>Adjustment>Hue/Saturation and select 'Colorize' and use the sliders.

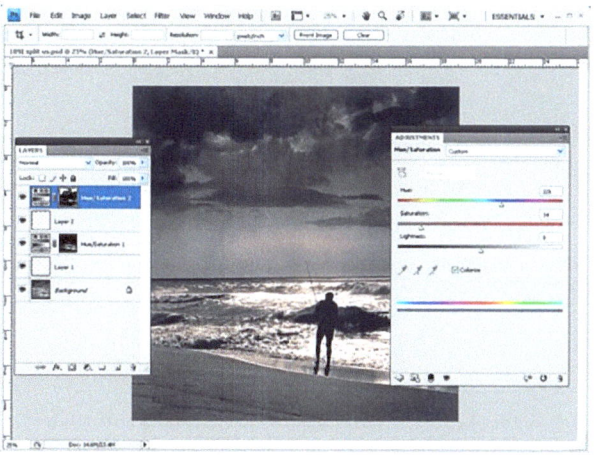

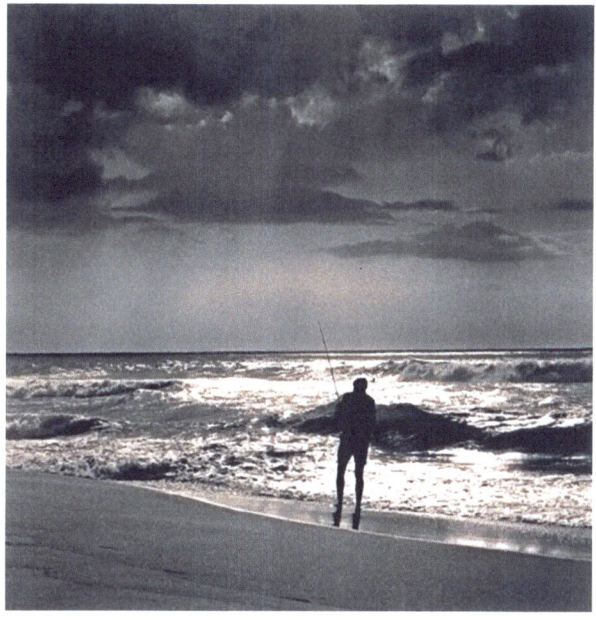

Selenium

The simulation of selenium toner gave me the most trouble. My attempts to produce the rich blacks that a bath of dilute selenium, that smelly and not good for your health chemical, produced in my darkroom were thwarted time and time again. But, perseverance does pay and I eventually came up with a result that seemed to work.

I opened my black and white image and made a new Hue/Saturation Adjustment Layer. I then began using the hue slider until I ended up with a reasonable looking colour at 220. I then reduced the saturation to 11 and sighed with relief as I viewed the image and gave an even bigger sigh when the print came out of the printer. These settings gave me the richer blacks I was after but if you want more of the plum colour that was a result of using a stronger mixture of selenium then try a Hue setting around the 250 mark.

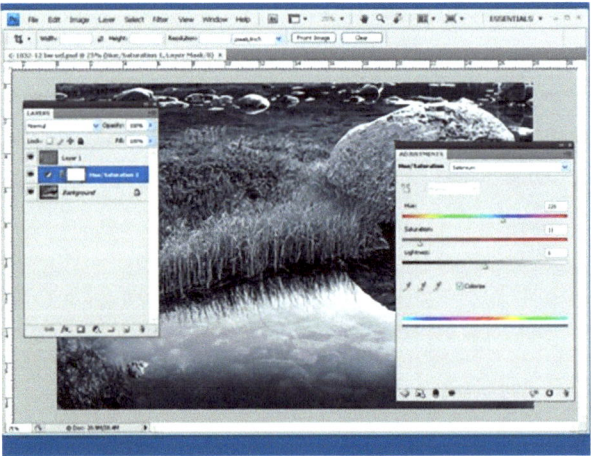

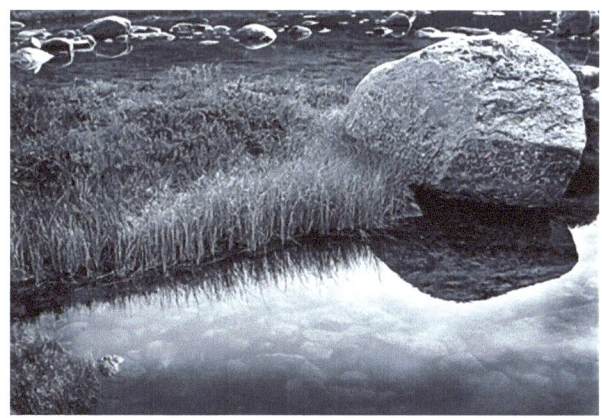

Lith Printing

Lith printing in the darkroom was something I had never aspired to. It is, I am told, a process that depends on many variables including the strength and freshness of the developer and that no two prints from the same negative are identical. However, some of the results I have seen have been stunning so I decided to have a go at simulating the effect in Photoshop.

Lith prints are distinguishable by the graininess of the shadows, the appearance of pinkish tones in highlights and the contrast that comes from an overexposed paper that is developed for a long time in quite dilute developer and whipped from the developer before development is complete.

After scouring the internet and trying out a number of suggested processes, I finally achieved a reasonable result following this procedure. I opened my black and white image and increased its contrast by using a Curves Adjustment Layer to darken the shadows and brighten the highlights. On a second Curves Adjustment Layer I selected the red channel and anchored a point near the bottom of the curve and again near the middle before clicking near the top and moving the curve upwards until I had a colour I was happy with. I then selected the green channel and anchored it as before and clicked near the top and moved the curve upwards to fine tune the colour.

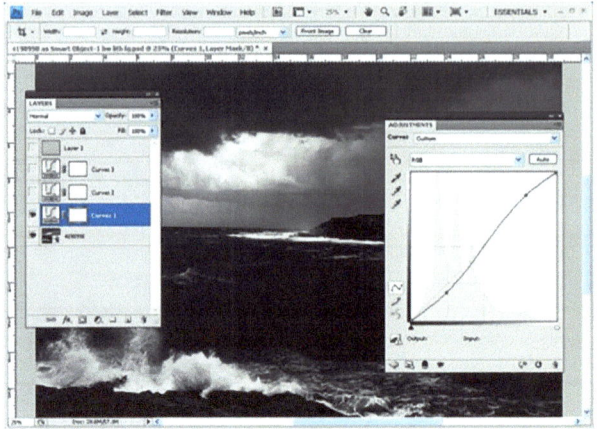

To provide the grain for the shadows, I opened a new Adjustment Layer, changed its Blend Mode to 'Overlay' and filled it with 50% grey (Edit> Fill). I then went to Filters>Noise>Add Noise which I added at 140 after making sure that Monochrome and Gaussian Blur were selected. To get rid of the grain in the highlights —at present it was over the whole image — I double clicked on the thumbnail on the Adjustment Layer which brought up a dialogue box. I went to the 'Blend if' section and moved the slider at the right hand end of the 'Underlying layer' to the left to 227 and then held down the Option key and moved the left half of that slider to 111. This smoothes the transition between dark and light.

Having done this, I felt that the grain was too overpowering so deleted the Adjustment Layer and opened a new one and, as before, changed its Blend Mode to 'Overlay' and filled it with 50% grey (Edit> Fill). I then went to Filters>Artistic>Film Grain and put in 'Grain 9, Highlight area 6, Intensity 6'. I was much happier with this and, after tweaking a new Curves layer to increase definition in the light clouds, all that was left was to go to the 'Blend if' section and set the 'Underlying layer' to 221 and 111.

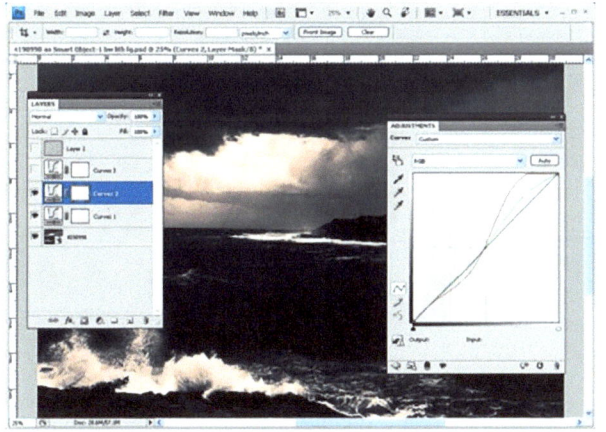

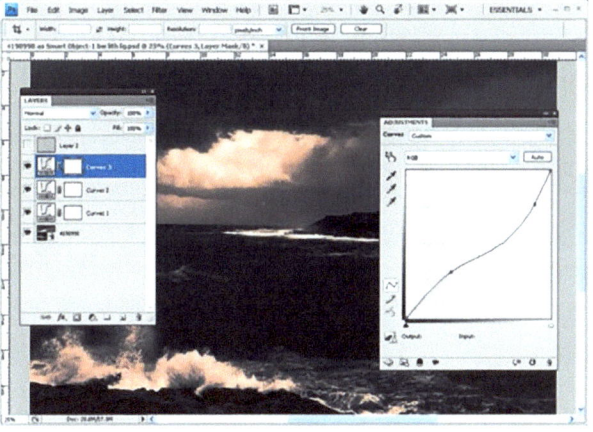

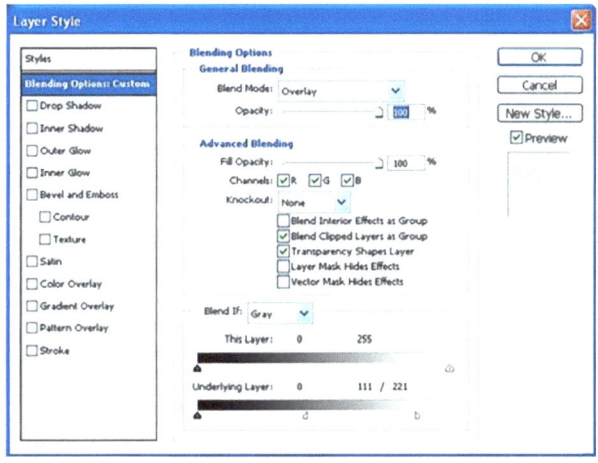

37

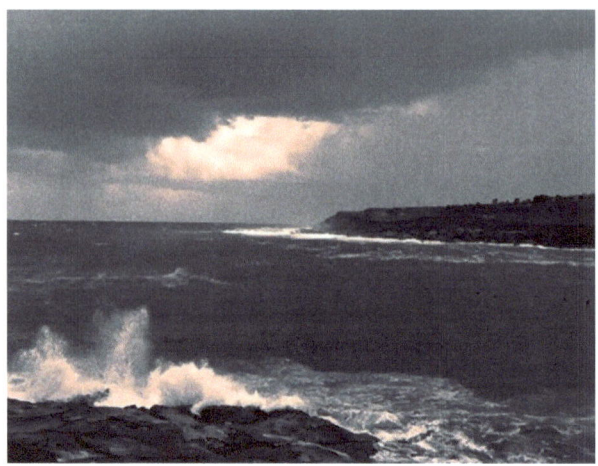

Photoshop can produce much of what we did in the darkroom and if you are a black and white enthusiast then I encourage you to have a go at finding out just what can be done to enhance your monochrome images.

Magic with Photoshop

I didn't really abandon my darkroom. It was just that I couldn't take it with me when I moved house. Darkrooms, from the early makeshift in the family bathroom to my purpose built palace under the house with permanent blackout and two enlargers, had been part of my life since at fourteen I first watched a photograph come to life in a tray of developer. It was then that I felt the magic of a darkroom and was hooked. I knew then that I wanted to learn how to conjure images from a negative onto a piece of paper.

For many years I did that and enjoyed many happy hours — and some frustrating ones — sloshing papers around in chemicals in the dark or at least in the red glow of my safelight.

But, without my darkroom I had to confine myself to transparency film. As a freelance writer and photographer that was fine as publishers and photo libraries required images to be on that medium. But then came computers and scanners and CDs and Photoshop and thoughts of how to set up another darkroom faded as my enlargers lay untouched in the garage. Publishers stopped wanting transparencies but now asked for digital files on a CD — most publishers anyway — so by stealth, digital began taking over my life. I still shot on film but even that was on the slippery slide and, after a period of resistance, I invested in a DSLR and Photoshop became even more important to me.

But, does Photoshop give me the same thrill, the same magic that I experienced in the darkroom? In many ways it does. My concern is with the finished product and I'm not overly concerned how it is achieved. I still feel excited when an image that I have created begins to look like the scene that I saw when I lifted the camera to my eye. The fact that it is appearing on a monitor rather than in a tray of developer is immaterial to me.

And, some exciting things can happen with Photoshop just as they did in the conventional darkroom.

Nearly all of my work with Photoshop just replicates what I had previously done in a darkroom and I therefore use only a fraction of the many possibilities that the program provides. However, I do spend some of my spare time fiddling with the less familiar aspects of Photoshop for my own enjoyment. A bit like my Sunday afternoon sessions in the darkroom when I experimented with various techniques and sometimes produced some unexpected results. In fact, several versions of Photoshop ago I made a mistake while fiddling which led me to an unexpected sale and showed me some of the magic of the new technology. That is if you can call a mistake magic.

I was scanning some black and white negatives and all had gone well until I came to one that had produced prints that had been successful in several exhibitions around Australia with a couple of Highly Commended awards. Onto the scanner it went (a Microtek flatbed) and eventually the image appeared on the computer screen. I scanned at the highest resolution (on that scanner it is 2400dpi) in RGB mode even though the negative was monochrome as I find that this generally gives the best results. I then use the various controls to adjust the image.

On this occasion I was using the Curves control and obviously wasn't concentrating as all of a sudden my monochrome image started appearing with colour. It didn't look bad so I began experimenting and ended up producing an image that looked as if it had been shot on transparency film and then developed in colour negative chemicals. I was so taken with the result that I submitted it to a digital photography magazine and it was published under the heading 'Who needs cross processing?'.

Later, I decided to see how the mistake had occurred so I took another monochrome negative and scanned it. I opened the Curves control and started adjusting but nothing produced any colour. Of course it wouldn't because I was working with all the RGB channels together. As soon as I switched to the Red channel alone things began to happen. Then I played with the Green and the Blue and back to the Red and so on. This is not a scientific process — at least the way I do it isn't. It's all trial and error but, to me, it's as good as messing about in the darkroom.

Here is an example of what I am writing about. I scanned my black and white negative and then opened it in Photoshop and began playing. The steps I followed were:

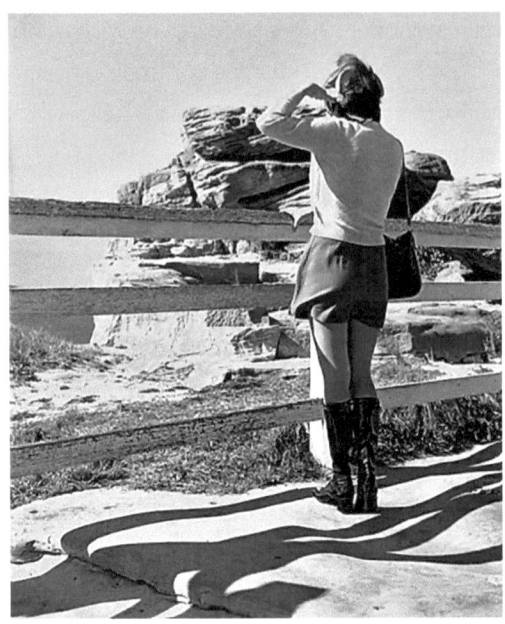

1 I made a small adjustment in a Curves layer to the Red and Green channels and then another small adjustment to the RGB channel.

2 I made a fairly large adjustment in a new Curves layer to the Red channel.

3 In a new Curves layer I made a large adjustment to the Green channel and a medium adjustment to the RGB channel.

4 In a new Curves layer I made large adjustments to the Blue and RGB channels.

5 I adjusted the Midtone of the Green in a Color Balance layer.

6 In the Master channel in a Hue/Saturation layer I adjusted the Saturation and Hue.

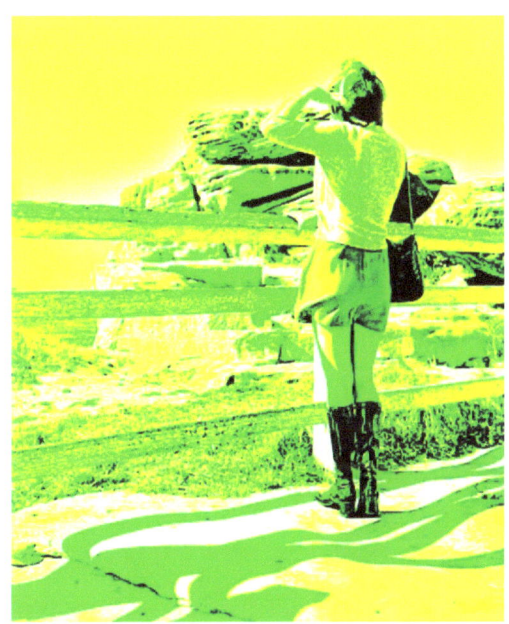

The curves that I ended up with were, at times, quite unusual to say the least but all I was after was to see what happened and you should do the same. After I had saved the green and yellow image I went further with my experiment and clicked on 'Colorize' in a new Hue/Saturation layer and, with no further adjustments, the result is shown below. Then, as the bug had bitten me, I tried a whole new set of adjustments on the same print and came up with a completely different image.

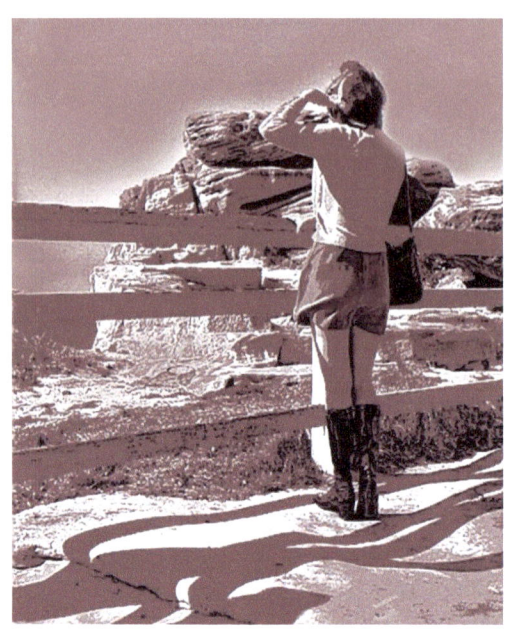

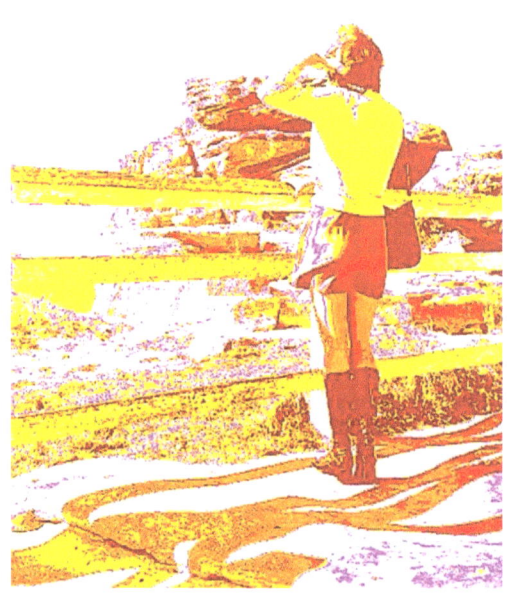

And, what use is this technique? To begin with it enables you to produce some different results from your negatives (or, of course, from your digitally captured images). In my case as a freelance, it enables me to produce some strikingly different images that can be used by publishers as generic illustrations to draw a reader's attention to an article (see below).

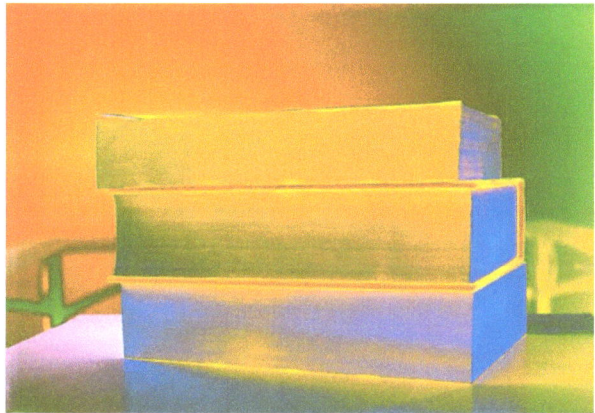

Whether you use this technique is neither here nor there but I hope that you can see that there are untold opportunities to experiment with black and white on the computer just as there are in the darkroom.

About the Author

David Bigwood is a regularly published writer and photographer with his work having been used in well over sixty publications, mainly in Australia and the United Kingdom.

He has qualified as a Licentiate of the Royal Photographic Society and is a member of the Australian Society of Authors.

He is a columnist for the UK magazine *F2 Freelance Photographer* and has written for *Australian Photography, Australian Camera* and *Better Photography.*

He founded and edited *The Black and White Enthusiast* magazine (later *Silvershotz*) and was sometime editor of the *Journal of the Australian Photographic Society.*

He has images with Alamy, the on-line photography library.

His prints, many of them in black and white, hang in private collections in Australia, Canada, England and the Cayman Islands and are available at davidbigwood.zenfolio.com

www.ingramcontent.com/pod-product-compliance
Lightning Source LLC
Chambersburg PA
CBHW041112180526
45172CB00001B/215